Army ants attack

by Clint Twist

Copyright © ticktock Entertainment Ltd 2006
First published in Great Britain in 2006 by ticktock Media Ltd.,
Unit 2, Orchard Business Centre, North Farm Road, Tunbridge Wells, Kent, TN2 3XF
ISBN 1 86007 839 7 PB Printed in China
A CIP catalogue record for this book is available from the British Library.
Picture Credits
Alamy: 19t (Danita Delimont), 19 side panel (Soren Breiting). Alex Wild (www.myrmecos.net): 2-3, 4, 4-5, 5, 5 side
panel, 8-9, 10, 17 side panel, 19b. FLPA: 8, 16 (Norbert Wu/Minden Picture), 9 side panel, 13b (Mark Moffett/Minden
Pictures). Getty Images: 25b (George Grall). NHPA: 9t (George Bernard), 23 (Adrian Hepworth). OSF: 16-17. Premaphotos
Wildlife: 1, 15 side panel (Ken Preston-Mafham). Science Photo Library: 12 (Mona Lisa Production),13 side panel (Dr
Morley Read), 15t, 21 (George Bernard), 14-15 (Sinclair Stammers), 26 (Jean-Phillipe Varin/Jacana), 7 side panel
(Volker Steger).

Every effort has been made to trace the copyright holders, and we apologise in advance for any unintentional omissions.
We would be pleased to insert the appropriate acknowledgements in any subsequent edition of this publication.

CONTENTS

What is an Army Ant?

Army ants are small insects. Army ants go on the march in very large numbers, with more than a million of them in a single column.

How do they live?

Army ants are carnivores – they eat other animals, mainly other minibeasts. They are predators that hunt, catch, and kill their prey, and also scavengers, that feed on the bodies of dead animals.

Where do they live?

Army ants are found in tropical forests in South and Central America and in Africa. Those that live in Africa are sometimes called driver ants.

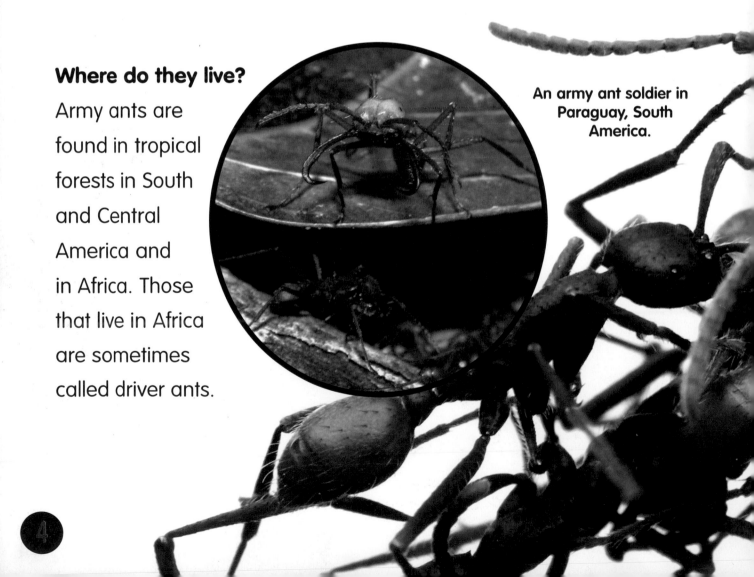

An army ant soldier in Paraguay, South America.

All ants belong to an insect group known as the social insects because they prefer to live in large family groups known as colonies.

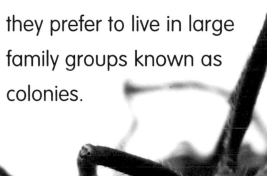

Understanding minibeasts

Insects belong to a group of minibeasts known as arthropods. Adult arthropods have jointed legs but do not have an inner skeleton made of bones. Instead, they have a tough outer "skin" called an exoskeleton. All insects have six legs when they are adults, and most also have at least one pair of wings, although some have two pairs.

All ants belong to a group of minibeasts known as arthropods.

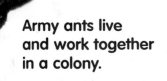

Army ants live and work together in a colony.

5

An Army Ant Up Close

A typical army ant worker is about 8-15 mm long with very thin legs and no wings. The ant's outer covering (exoskeleton) is very tough.

An army ant is an insect, with the same parts of the body as all other adult insects. It has three parts: head, thorax, and abdomen.

The head is made up of a brain, a mouth, and a pair of antennae. Some army ants also have eyes, but most are completely blind.

The head of an army ant.

Army ants, like all other insects, have three parts to their bodies.

The abdomen is largest part of the body and contains the stomach and other important organs.

The thorax is the thinnest part of the body and the ant's three pairs of legs are attached here.

Six legs

Ants and other insects are sometimes called hexapods because they all have six legs (hex means six in Latin). This is correct, but it is not completely accurate. All insects are hexapods, but not all hexapods are insects. Some other minibeasts, such as springtails, have six legs but they are not insects.

A springtail has six legs but is not an insect. Ants also have six legs and they are insects.

Roving colony

An insect colony is a single family of closely related insects. A big colony would have as many as 20 million ants, but most have between one and two million ants.

A single army ant eats only a tiny amount of food each day, but if you add up all the food needed for each ant, it becomes a very large amount.

An army ant colony, such as this one in Panama which is sweeping the forest floor for prey, needs a lot of food to survive.

This huge appetite means that the colony has to keep moving in order to find new supplies of food. If the colony does not keep moving it will quickly starve and die.

An army ant colony at rest in a hollow tree in Costa Rica.

Army ants do not keep moving all the time. They have a regular stop-start cycle that lasts for about 35 days. There are 15 days of non-stop marching followed by 20 days when the colony stops.

A colony of army ants pulling apart a cricket.

Crammed with life

The tropical forests of Central and South America and Africa are completely crammed with life. There are more species of minibeasts in these forests than anywhere else on Earth. These hot, wet forests are the only places that produce enough food for army ants. That is why army ants are not found anywhere else.

A tiger moth being attacked by army ants.

Family Members

Every colony contains up to four types of army ant. Three of the types – queen, worker, and soldier – are in the colony at all times. A fourth type of army ant – the male – only appears at certain times.

In each colony there is a fertile female that is known as the queen. The queen is the largest in size (about 30-50 mm) and her most important job is to lay eggs.

A queen army ant with a worker riding on her back.

The rest of the full-time members of the colony are sterile females. Most of these are workers that spend all their time collecting food and carrying it back to the colony.

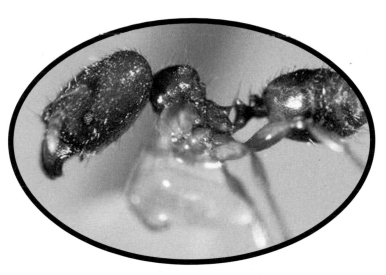

Soldier army ants have eyes to detect predators and prey.

The army ant soldiers are larger females up to 25 mm long, which have special weapons to kill prey and to defend the workers and the queen. Some of the soldiers are the only ants in the colony apart from the queen that have eyes.

Worker army ants make up the majority of the colony.

Fearsome weapons

Army ant soldiers are not just bigger and stronger than the workers; they also have lots of minibeast weapons. Their heads and jaws are huge, and their main method of attack is a fearsome charge head-on. The solder ants of some species also have a sting at the end of the abdomen, while others can squirt a spray of poisonous formic acid.

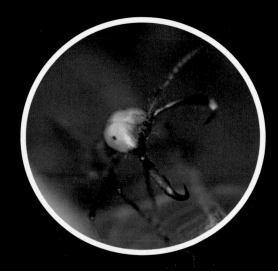

Soldiers have impressive weapons to protect against and attack enemies.

Blind obedience

All of the army ant workers are completely blind. The only way they can sense the outside world is by feeling vibrations with their legs and by detecting smells with their antennae.

The antennae detect chemicals known as pheromones that are made by the other ants in the colony.

It is the job of the small number of soldiers that do have eyes to feed the colony's constant hunger. Using their sense of sight, these soldiers lead scout parties that search for food.

The blue circle in the centre of the head is this army ant soldier's eye.

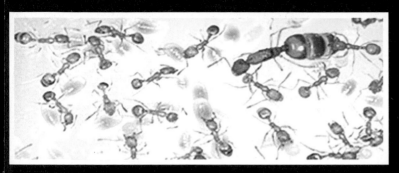

Ants use pheromones to communicate with each other.

When the scouts find food, they lay a trail of pheromones back to the colony. Workers then follow the trail and collect the food while the scout party carries on looking.

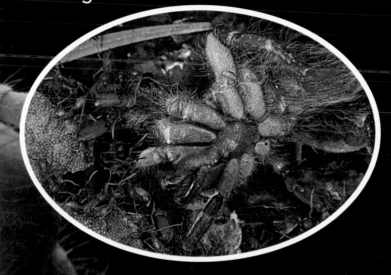

Army ants, like this colony in Peru, can attack a creature as big as a tarantula.

If the army ant workers encounter any difficulty (such as a predator with a taste for ants) they release alarm pheromones that quickly attract soldiers to the scene.

Central control

The queen controls the activity of the whole colony through a set of special "command pheromones" that only queens can make. Some of these special pheromones are used to control the other ants, such as making sure that scouts are sent out to find enough food. Other pheromones are used to tell the colony when it is time to stop and rest.

The queen uses her pheromones to tell the colony to stop and rest.

Raiding Parties

When the ants are on the move, the whole colony marches through the forest like a living river. This river moves through the forest at a very slow speed, eating everything in its path.

An army ant stealing a larva of a pavement ant.

When the colony stops, most of the colony stays still while a raiding party is sent out each day. Each raiding party contains up to 600,000 insects.

A raiding party is sent out in a different direction every day until all the available food has been collected. It is then time for the colony to move on.

These worker ants are pulling apart this gryllid cricket in Costa Rica.

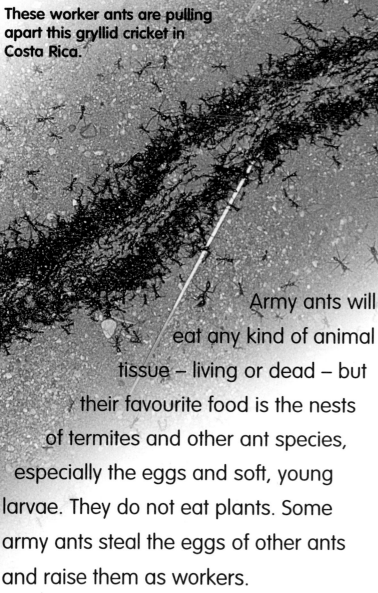

Army ants will eat any kind of animal tissue – living or dead – but their favourite food is the nests of termites and other ant species, especially the eggs and soft, young larvae. They do not eat plants. Some army ants steal the eggs of other ants and raise them as workers.

Food processing

Although army ant workers are blind, they are extremely efficient at collecting food. The workers use pheromones fo communicate with other ants. They work together to carry prey that is too heavy for a single ant to carry. They may also cut up the prey with their sharp jaws and carry it back in pieces.

Army ants carrying small prey back to their nest in Trinidad.

close community

When they come to a stop, they form a very tightly packed community. They link their bodies to form a living home that can cling onto any surface.

Army ants using their bodies to build a bridge for other ants to walk across in Panama.

A colony of army ants does not need very much shelter from the weather because it can provide its own. All that the colony needs is a branch or a fallen log to provide some support for the combined weight of a million or so ants.

The building process starts with the strongest ants: the soldiers. They grab hold of each other to make chains.

Army ants link their bodies to make a strong structure to build a nest.

The nest is made stronger by the bodies of thousands of workers that fill in all the gaps around the outside of the colony.

Inside the nest, thousands more workers link their bodies to make spaces for the queen and the eggs. The fiercest and best-armed soldiers take up guard duty on the outside.

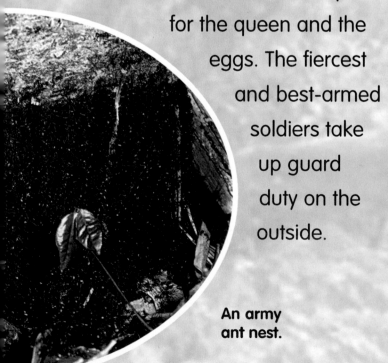

An army ant nest.

River crossing

Ants cannot swim, and they are so small that the slightest current can carry them away. But that does not stop them crossing streams and rivers. Soldiers and workers can use their bodies to create a temporary "living bridge" across a small stream. For larger stretches of water, the ants link their bodies to create "living rafts" that can float the colony across.

By building a bridge with their bodies, army ants can cross any gap in their path.

Queen Ant

The queen ant is the most important ant in the whole colony. All the others can be replaced, but there is only one queen. The main task of the queen is to lay eggs that will hatch into new workers.

A queen army ant mates only once at the beginning of her adult life. But a queen army ant does not lay eggs every day.

The queen does not lay eggs while the colony is moving. The timing of her egg-laying happens when the colony rests.

Once the queen lays her eggs, the colony rests.

Army ants layer themselves on top of one another to protect the eggs inside the nest, such as this one in Panama.

It is a special pheromone made by the queen while she is laying eggs that tells the colony to stay in one place. As soon as egg-laying stops, the queen stops making that pheromone; the workers and soldiers unlink their bodies, and the colony moves on.

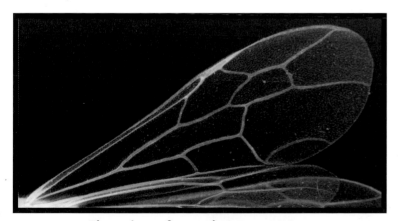

The wing of a male army ant.

When the colony reaches its biggest size, the queen will lay special queen and male eggs. When these eggs hatch, the males and the new queens fly away to start new colonies.

Flying ants

The only army ants that have wings are queens and males, which are only born about once every two years. The queen ants fly away to mate and establish new colonies. After a queen has mated she always chews off her wings as she doesn't need them anymore. The males also fly away to find queens to mate with. They are much bigger than the flying queens and are sometimes called "sausage flies". After mating, the males soon die.

A male sausage fly in Gambia, West Africa.

Raising the Young

Young army ants get very special care. In fact the workers spend as much time and effort to caring for the young as they do to collecting food.

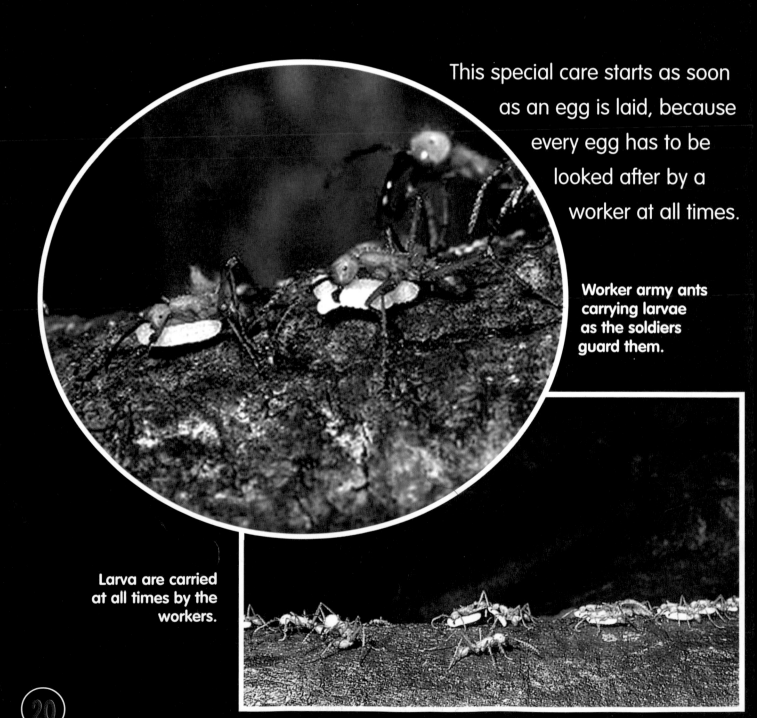

This special care starts as soon as an egg is laid, because every egg has to be looked after by a worker at all times.

Worker army ants carrying larvae as the soldiers guard them.

Larva are carried at all times by the workers.

When the eggs hatch, the workers also have to carry around and care for the ant larvae. The amount of work increases because the larvae have to be fed. The workers chew food for the larvae to make it easy for them to digest.

Worker ants carrying larvae and pupae across the forest floor in Costa Rica.

It is only after the larvae have gone through pupation and have become adults that they are able to feed themselves and begin working for the colony.

Insect development

Insects develop from eggs in two different ways. With many kinds of insect, including ants, bees, and beetles, the eggs hatch into larvae that look very different from the adults. The larvae go through a stage called pupation when they change into adults. However, with many other kinds of insect, such as cockroaches and grasshoppers, the eggs hatch into nymphs that already have the adult body shape.

Army ants go through several stages to become adults.

Army Ants & Humans

The idea of army ants is terrifying – a living river of insects that flows through the forest eating every animal in its path, and is absolutely unstoppable. However, despite their scary reputation, army ants are not really harmful to humans.

Even when walking at a slow pace, humans can move much faster than army ants. So people who live or work in tropical forests have no difficulty getting out of the ants' way.

People welcome army ant invasions to their homes in tropical rainforests.

Army ants on the hunt for food.

Animals that cannot move, such as chickens in coops or goats tethered to the ground, are in big trouble. The ants quickly swarm up their legs and over their whole bodies. When the ants begin feeding, the victims usually die from loss of blood.

Army ants eating a scorpion in Corcovado National Park, Costa Rica.

Many people who live in tropical forests actually welcome the arrival of army ants. Not only do the ants eat any insect pests living there, they also eat all the dead insects that have collected in corners and underneath furniture. A visit from army ants is like a "spring cleaning" session.

Welcome disturbance

The arrival of an army ant colony is good news for some animals. As the army ants get closer and closer many large insects, such as cockroaches and beetles, come out of hiding and try to escape. These insects may be fast enough to run away from the slow-moving ants, but they are likely to be spotted by larger predators. Some birds follow army ants to catch the large insects that are driven out by them.

A bicoloured antbird from Costa Rica, which follows ants in order to catch food.

Different Behaviours

While army ants are constantly on the move, other woodland ant species follow a much more settled existence.

Wood ants

Wood ants are so-called as they live in woods and forests in places with a warm climate. Colonies of wood ants build their nests completely underground beneath the forest floor out of fallen leaves and woodland debris. In the cooler regions, they often construct a mound above the nest. These mounds can be up to one metre in height.

Acacia ants

In areas that are too dry for thick forest, some ants build their nests at the base of thorny trees such as the acacia. The ants feed on nectar made by the tree, and they keep the tree clear of other insects. If any other animal tries to eat the acacia tree, the ants rush along the branches to bite and sting the "attacker".

Leafcutter ants

Leafcutter ants cut out pieces of leaf and carry them back to their underground nest. The ants line their tunnels with these bits of leaf and allow a fungus to grow on them. This fungus provides these ants with a steady supply of food.

Ants milking aphids

Some ants, such as common garden ants, get their food by feeding on other insects. Many plants attract small sap-sucking insects known as aphids. Garden ants have learned to stroke these aphids while they are feeding. This makes the aphids produce a sweet-sticky substance known as honeydew, which the ants love to eat.

Unusual Ants

There are about 10,000 different species of ant. Most of them are instantly recognizable as ants, although a few are a lot more unusual.

Replete ants

Bees are not the only insects that make and store honey. Some ant species collect nectar from flowers and feed it to special workers that are known as repletes. Replete ants store this excess food and in times of need, it is regurgitated for the other ants to eat. A replete ant can swell up to the size of a grape.

Velvet ant

Despite its name, this "ant" is in fact a species of wasp that sneaks into bumblebee colonies and lays its eggs on their larvae. When the wasp eggs hatch, the wasp larvae eat the bee larvae.

Argentine ant

During the last 100 years, Argentine ants have sneaked aboard ships and planes hidden in cargo and have spread to almost every country in the world. They have become a pest because they are one of the few ant species that can survive inside modern heated buildings.

Fire ant

These red-coloured ants were once found only in the hot, wet forests of South America, but they have been accidentally introduced to other countries hidden in shipments of timber and have become a serious pest. Fire ants have a sting that injects a very strong poison that can kill young farm animals.

Find out More
Lifecycle

Army ant eggs are microscopic and white or yellowish in colour. The eggs hatch into larva which do not have eyes or legs. The larva builds a cocoon around itself and changes into the pupa. When the pupa leaves its cocoon, it becomes an adult ant.

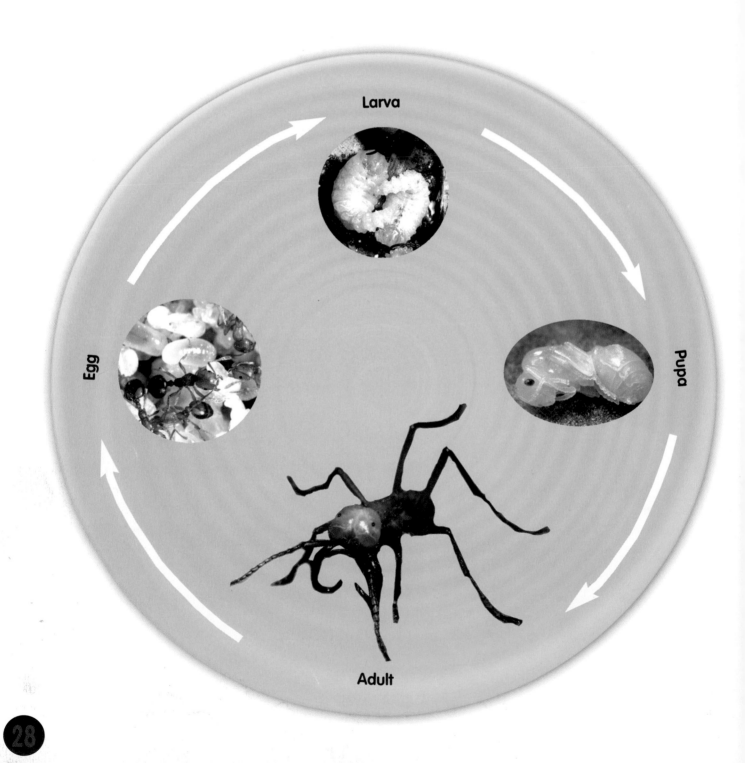

Larva

Egg

Pupa

Adult

Fabulous Facts

Fact 1: A colony of army ants can kill and eat up to 100,000 animals (mostly insects) in a day!

Fact 2: Army ants can climb trees and eat birds.

Fact 3: The queen only needs to mate once to produce eggs for the rest of her life.

Fact 4: After a male army ant mates with the queen, he dies within 48 hours.

Fact 5: Workers live for several months, while the queen may live up to several years.

Fact 6: Although army ants have a painful sting, they do not come into contact with humans that often.

Fact 7: Army ants have been known to kill and eat as large an animal as a horse!

Fact 8: If you gathered up all the humans in the world and all the ants, they would weigh the same.

Fact 9: In some species of African army ant (driver ants) the queen produces eggs daily (up to four million a month).

Fact 10: Army ants can only swallow liquid; they have to spit out solid food.

Fact 11: The army ant species existed at the time of dinosaurs, 100 million years ago, and have not changed since then.

Fact 12: There are approximately 150 species of army ant found mostly in Central and South America.

Fact 13: Army ants travel roughly one metre per minute whilst marching.

Glossary

Abdomen – the largest part of an insect's three-part body: the abdomen, contains most of the important organs.

Antennae – a pair of special sense organs found at the front of the head on most insects.

Arthropod – any minibeast that has jointed legs; insects and spiders are arthropods.

Carnivore – an animal that eats meat.

Caterpillar – a butterfly or moth larva.

Colony – a group of insects, or other living things, which live very closely together.

Cycle – a series of repeated events that follow a regular pattern.

Digestive system – the organs that are used to process food.

Driver ants – army ants that live in Africa.

Formic acid – substance produced by some ants that causes skin irritation and chemical burns.

Exoskeleton – a hard outer covering that protects and supports the bodies of some minibeasts.

Honey – sweet, syrupy substance produced by honeybees and some ants.

Insect – a kind of minibeast that has six legs, most insects also have wings.

Larva – a wormlike creature that is the juvenile (young) stage in the life cycle of many insects.

Minibeast – one of a large number of small land animals that do not have a skeleton.

Nectar – a sweet sugary substance produced by flowering plants and used by honeybees and some ants to make honey.

Nymph – the juvenile (young) stage in the life cycle of insects that do not produce larvae.

Organ – a part of an animal's body that performs a particular task, e.g. the heart pumps blood.

Parasite – any living thing that lives or feeds on or in the body of another living thing.

Pedicel – the narrow "waist" of an ant at the top of the abdomen where it meets the thorax.

Predator – an animal that hunts and eats other animals.

Prey – an animal that is eaten by other animals.

Pupa – An insect larva that is in the process of turning into an adult.

Pupation – the process by which insect larvae change their body shape to the adult form.

Queen – the largest army ant in a colony; the queen is the only female army ant that can lay eggs.

Regurgitate – to bring up partially digested food.

Replete – a special kind of ant worker that stores honey inside its body.

Scavenger – an animal that eats dead and rotting plants and animals.

Skeleton – an internal structure of bones that supports the bodies of large animals such as mammals, reptiles, and fish.

Soldier – a sterile female army ant that is larger than a worker; most soldiers have weapons such as stings and poison to attack prey and defend the colony.

Thorax – the middle part of an insect's body where the legs are attached.

Tropical – belonging to the region around the Earth's equator where the climate is always hot.

Worker – a sterile female army ant, nearly all the army ants in a colony are workers.

index